Max Hodes, who also compiled *The Official Scottish Joke Book*, writes an entertaining column called 'Chatalong With Max' in the *Daily Record*, Scotland's biggest-selling daily newspaper. The *Record*'s advertising slogan is 'You Just Can't Put It Down', in contrast to *The World's Worst Joke Book* – 'You Just Can't Pick It Up'.

Also by Max Hodes:

THE OFFICIAL SCOTTISH JOKE BOOK

Also available:

THE OFFICIAL IRISH JOKE BOOK
THE OFFICIAL IRISH JOKE BOOK NO. 3 (BOOK 2 TO FOLLOW)
POSITIVELY THE LAST IRISH JOKE BOOK

Edited by Max Hodes

The World's
Worst Joke Book

Illustrated by Lorne Brown

Futura

A *Futura* BOOK

First published in Great Britain by
Futura Publications Limited in 1979
Reprinted 1980, 1984

*To Jeannette
the world's best listener*

ISBN 0 7088 1605 3

Printed in Great Britain by
Hazell Watson & Viney Limited,
Member of the BPCC Group,
Aylesbury, Bucks

ACKNOWLEDGEMENTS

The Editor wishes to acknowledge the help of Jack
McLaughlin, Andy Cameron, Clem Dane, Tony Goodman,
Gordon Irving, and the makers of Christmas crackers
everywhere.

Futura Publications
A Division of
Macdonald & Co (Publishers) Ltd
Maxwell House
74 Worship Street
London EC2A 2EN
A BPCC plc Company

'Waiter, what soup is this?'
'It's bean soup, sir.'
'Never mind what it was, I want to know what it is now.'

Why do bakers work so hard?
Because they knead the dough.

'Doctor, doctor, I've lost my memory.'
'When did this happen?'
'When did what happen?'

Why do bees hum?
Because they don't know the words.

'Nurse, I'm at death's door.'
'Don't worry – the doctor will pull you through.'

What did the big chimney say to the little chimney?
You're too young to smoke.

Hear about the psychiatrist who kept his wife
under the bed?
He thought she was a little potty.

'Do you like bathing beauties?'
'I don't know – I've never bathed one.'

What are two rows of cabbages called?
A dual cabbage-way.

'Are you dancing?'
'Are you asking?'
'I'm asking!'
'I'm dancing.'

'Waiter, what's wrong with these eggs?'
'Don't ask me – I only laid the table.'

'Knock-knock.'
'Who's there?'
'Atch.'
'Atch who?'
'Sorry, I didn't know you had a cold.'

How long is the next bus?
Oh, about eighteen feet.

Then there was the man in hospital who took a turn for the nurse.

A dry cleaner was excused from jury duty the other day because he claimed his business was very pressing.

'My dog has no nose.'
'How does it smell?'
'Terrible.'

'Abie, I heard you had a big fire at the shop.'
'Sssh! It's not till *next* week.'

'Waiter, there's a dead fly in my soup.'
'Yes, it's the hot water that kills them.'

WARD 4
MATERNITY
LORNE

Then there was the man who lost his health because he was always drinking the health of others.

And how about the woman who decided to have only three children? She heard that one in every four children born is Chinese.

Nurse to expectant dad: 'First the good news – you're top of the housing list.'

Policeman: 'This happens to be a one-way street.' Motorist: 'That's all right – I'm only going one way.'

The nicest thing about money is that it never clashes with anything you're wearing.

Hear about the Irishman who drove his car into a lake? He was trying to dip the headlights.

Marriage is like a three-ring circus. First the
engagement ring, then the wedding ring and,
finally, the suffering.

Army recruit: 'What happens if the 'chute fails to
open?'
Instructor: 'Bring it back and we'll give you
another.'

Bulldog for sale. Eats anything. Very fond of
children.

Judge: 'After taking everything into considera-
tion, I'm going to award your wife £5 a week.'
Defendant: 'That's very kind, your honour. And
I might even slip her a pound or two myself.'

Did you hear about the poor little bloater that
went deaf? All his mates clubbed together and
bought him a herring aid.

'How did you find your steak?' asked the waiter.
'I just moved a chip, and there it was,' replied
the customer.

On which ship did the first insects sail to America?
The Mayfly.

'Doctor, I feel like a pair of curtains.'
'Well, pull yourself together.'

'I just got a beautiful French poodle for my wife.'
'I wish I could get a trade-in like that.'

Then there was the Eskimo wife who complained
her husband didn't get home till half-past Feb-
ruary.

Did you hear about the private who won the V.C.
for saving his company during the invasion of
Normandy?
He shot the cook.

Why did the chicken cross the road?
For some fowl reason.

'Dad, there's a man at the door with a moustache.'
'Tell him I've got one.'

What did the ghost say to the barman?
Do you serve spirits here?

'Will you bounce up and down on your bed, please?'
'Why, nurse?'
'I forgot to shake the bottle before I gave you your medicine.'

'I've had my dog put down.'
'Was it mad?'
'Well, it wasn't too pleased.'

Did you hear about the two thirsty snails who went on a pub crawl?

'Knock-knock.'
'Who's there?'
'Cook.'
'Cook who?'
'That's the first one I've heard this year.'

Policeman: 'You were doing 50mph.'
Motorist: 'Would you mind putting 90mph on the summons? Then I can show it to the man I'm trying to sell this car to.'

'Doctor, about those tablets you gave me to build up my strength – well, I can't get the lid off the bottle.'

'Once a week, I like to take a bath in milk.'
'Pasteurized?'
'No, just up to my neck.'

A man celebrates his birthday by taking a day off. A woman celebrates her birthday by taking a year off.

Dolly bird, from behind screen: 'I've taken all my clothes off. Where shall I put them?'
Doctor: 'On top of mine.'

How do you start a Teddy race?
Ready, Teddy, go.

How do you use an Egyptian doorbell?
Toot-and-come-in.

Woman chef requires post; will go on hot plate.

'Doctor, I'm very worried. No one will talk to me.'
'Next!'

'The police are looking for a man with one eye called McPherson.'
'What's his other eye called?'

How do you make a Swiss roll?
Push him off the top of an Alp.

What comes out of a wardrobe at 100mph?
Stirling Moth.

'Knock-knock.'
'Who's there?'
'A little old lady.'
'A little old lady who?'
'I didn't know you could yodel.'

Then there were the two nudists who decided to stay at home. It was Poppy Day.

'My wife is allergic to fur. Every time she sees a woman wearing a mink coat, she gets sick.'

'Anything you say may be held against you.'
'Olivia Newton-John.'

She was only a constable's daughter, but she let the chief inspector.

'Nurse, I'm sending you up a case of malnutrition.'
'Thanks, doctor, it'll make a change from Lucozade.'

'My wife's a real angel – she's always harping on about something.' 

What's the best thing to do if chased by an elephant?
Make a trunk call, and reverse the charge.

'I took my son-in-law into my clothing business, and yesterday I caught him kissing one of the models.'
'Well, so what?'
'You don't understand – I make *men's* clothes!'

'Waiter, this coffee tastes like mud.'
'Well, it was ground only ten minutes ago.'

Lorne

How do porcupines make love?
Very carefully.

'That's a strange pair of socks you've got on –
one blue and the other red.'
'I know – I've another pair like that at home.'

'Nurse, did you tell Mr Duncan he's the father of
quads?'
'No, I didn't, doctor. He's still shaving.'

'You've got to help me, doctor. I keep thinking
I'm a bell.'
'Take these tablets three times a day. If you're no
better, give me a ring.'

A man walking in the park came across a penguin.
He took it to a policeman and asked what he
should do.
'Take it to the zoo,' replied the policeman.
Next day the policeman saw the man, still with
the penguin. 'Didn't I tell you to take that
penguin to the zoo?' he asked.
'That's what I did,' said the man. 'Today I'm
taking it to the pictures.'

Mr Newlywed to wife: 'Shall we go to bed now, or do you want to stay up and watch *Coronation Street*?'

Two flies on Kojak's head. Said one to the other: 'Smile – we're on Telly.'

Boss: 'You should have been here at nine o'clock this morning.'
Office boy: 'Why – what happened?'

'You were driving at 75mph, miss.'
'Isn't that marvellous, officer? And I only passed my test yesterday!'

The priest stopped a man walking down the road with a roll of cloth under his arm. 'Where did you get that?' he asked.
'I knocked it off,' the man replied.
'Well,' said the priest, 'I hope you're not going to make a habit of it.'
'No,' answered the man, 'a sports jacket.'

What team's football players have never met each other before the game?
Queen's Park Strangers.

'I'm afraid Philip has had to rush off to do an emergency operation.'
'A risky one?'
'Very – he's not even sure he'll get paid.'

'Knock-knock.'
'Who's there?'
'Irish stew.'
'Irish stew who?'
'Irish stew in the name of the law!'

My wife ought to have been a politician. She's always introducing new bills into the house.

Did you hear about the optician's daughter who went to a party? Two glasses and she made a spectacle of herself.

'Look here,' complained the Devil. 'You've only been in Hell a few days, yet you go around as if you owned the place.'
'Ah, but I do,' retorted the man. 'My mother-in-law gave it to me while I was alive.'

Did you hear about the millionaire flea who bought a pack of hounds.

Wife: 'It's absurd for this man to charge £15 for towing us two miles.'
Husband: 'That's all right – he's earning it. I've got my brakes on.'

What's the Bay City Rollers' favourite sweet?
Tartan custard.

Then there was the man who painted his car green on one side and yellow on the other. He loved to hear witnesses contradict each other.

We regret the incredible clairvoyant is unable to appear as billed tonight, due to unforeseen circumstances.

An Aberdeen pub offers free drinks to pensioners, providing they are accompanied by their parents.

What do you stuff a parrot with?
Pollyfilla.

'Waiter, these pancakes taste like polystyrene tiles.'
'Yes, sir, that's why we charge ceiling prices.'

'My wife say's she'll leave me if I don't give up following Rangers.'
'Oh, I'm sorry.'
'So am I. I'll miss her.'

Did you hear what happened to the man who couldn't tell putty from porridge? His windows fell out.

It takes over 3,000 bolts and screws to assemble a car – but it takes only one nut to scatter it all over the road.

'That shirt I bought for my husband has a hole in it. I want my money back.'
'Sorry, we don't give refunds.'
'But the notice in your window says "Money refunded if not satisfactory." '
'Sure, but there was nothing wrong with the money.'

'Will my measles be better next week, doctor?'
'Well, I hate to make rash promises.'

A Scotsman, an Englishman and a Jew had a six-course meal at an expensive restaurant.
When the waiter presented them with a bill for £50, the Scotsman said: 'I'll pay that.'
A headline in the next day's paper said: JEWISH VENTRILOQUIST FOUND DEAD IN ALLEY.

Hotel towels are the little things that are sent to dry us.

What a holiday we had. It only rained twice – once for three days and once for four.

'Mum, are you sure this is the way to make pizza?'
'Shut up and get back in the oven!'

'Waiter, there's a funny film on this soup.'
'What do you expect for 15p – *Star Wars*?'

'Doctor, I keep thinking I'm covered in gold.'
'Don't worry – it's just a gilt complex.'

'What do you know of the Ark?'
'Please, sir, it's what the Herald Angels sing.'

Some Irishmen are born losers. Paddy tried shoplifting – and stole a free sample.

Who has a parrot that shouts 'Pieces of four'?
Short John Silver.

Bookseller: 'This excellent book will do half your work.'
Schoolboy: 'I'll take two!'

'Help!' shouted the wife, as the gorilla hauled her into the bushes. 'What shall I do?'
'Same as you always do,' replied the husband. 'Tell him you've got a headache.'

Who is known as the Chiropodist King?
William the Corncurer.

Girl: 'I'm writing my life story.'
'How far have you got?'
'Chap 5.'

What did the bull sing to the cow?
When I fall in love, it will be for heifer.

Golfer: 'I'd move heaven and earth to break 100.'
Partner: 'Concentrate on heaven – you've moved
enough earth already.'

Man (at concert) 'Did I stand on your toes when
I went out?'
'Yes, you did.'
'Good – I'm back in the right seat.'

'That's a very small baby.'
'Well, we've only been married two weeks.'

What do you get if you cross a frog and a can of
cola?
Croak-a-cola.

Then there was the Aberdonian who gave his son
a pair of glasses, and told him to be sure to take
them off when he wasn't looking at anything.

'Waiter, do you serve crabs here?'
'We serve anyone – sit down!'

Hear about the clown who complained to the
garage that one of the doors of his car wouldn't
fall off?

'Knock-knock.'
'Who's there?'
'Martini.'
'Martini who?'
'Martini hands are frozen.'

One Christian to another, facing lions in ancient
Rome: 'One good thing – you don't get the crowds
running on to the pitch here.'

Why don't elephants eat penguins?
They can't get the wrappers off.

'Why do you call your dog Buttons?'
'He's often attached to trousers.'

LORNE

 Husband, phoning from pub: 'I know I said I'd be home after six, but I haven't finished my fourth yet.'

'Madam, this handkerchief is perfect. Why the complaint?'
'It was a sheet before I sent it to your laundry.'

Boxer: 'I'd like you to take a full-length picture of me.'
Photographer: 'Certainly, sir. When's your next fight?'

'How many people work in this office?'
'Oh, about half of them.'

Then there was the waiter christened 'Tomorrow' by his customers. He never comes.

'Why did you break off your engagement?'
'I saw him sunbathing, and he looked so different without his wallet.'

What did the mayonnaise say to the fridge?
Shut the door – I'm dressing.

'I say, I say – I used to be a tap dancer.'
'Why did you give it up?'
'I kept falling in the sink.'

Voice on phone: 'Jimmy won't be coming to school today. He's ill.'
Teacher: 'That's all right. Who's speaking?'
Voice: 'My father, sir.'

Then there was the psychiatrist who guaranteed his patients a cure – or their mania back.

Boss: 'Your salary is your own personal business – don't disclose it to anyone.'
Office boy: 'Don't worry, sir – I'm as ashamed of it as you are.'

Eskimo: 'Can I kiss your wife?'
'Sure – it's no skin off my nose.'

In Russia the only difference is that the television set watches you.

Then there was the Irishman who bought a music stool. He twisted and turned it, but couldn't get a note out of it.

'I'll have to charge you £5 for pulling out that tooth.'
'But you told me it would be only £1!'
'Yes, but you yelled so loudly, you scared away four other patients.'

'I went fishing with my wife yesterday.'
'Any luck?'
'No – I'm going back to using worms.'

A newspaper contest for the most unlikely head-line of the following year was won by: POPE ELOPES.

A Jewish boy and a Catholic boy were having an argument. The Catholic lad boasted: 'I'll bet our Father knows more than your Rabbi.'
'So he should,' retorted the Jewish lad. 'You tell him everything.'

'Doctor, doctor, everyone thinks I'm a liar.'
'I find that hard to believe.'

Mechanic: 'It'll take £150 to get this car purring again.'
Motorist: 'How much to get it to miaow a little?'

A golfer was taking a lot of trouble with his drive. His friend asked why.
'Well,' explained the golfer. 'I'm anxious to make this shot a really good one. My mother-in-law came with me today, and she's on the clubhouse verandah watching me.'
'Don't be a fool,' said his friend. 'You haven't a hope of hitting her from this distance.'

What fish terrorizes other fish?
Jack the Kipper.

A man rushed into an optician's just before closing time on a Saturday, saying: 'I've broken my glasses. Could you mend them for me?'

'Sorry,' replied the optician, 'I'm just about to close. But, if you like, I can board them up for you till Monday.'

Then there was the Irish tramp who found a drainpipe too hard for a pillow. So he stuffed it with straw.

'How do you like your new gas fire, Angus?'

'Great, Sandy. I lit it a fortnight ago and it hasn't gone out once.'

Hear about the farmer who couldn't keep his hands off his wife? So he sacked them all and bought a combine harvester.

Who invented vulgar fractions?

Henry the 1/8.

As two seagulls flew over a crowded Blackpool beach, one moaned: 'Takes all the skill out of it.'

Wife: 'I heard the downstairs clock strike two when you came home.'
'No, dear, it started to strike ten, but I held it back in case it woke you.'

'Sorry I'm late, sir. I sprained my ankle.'
'Huh! Another lame excuse.'

Where do policemen live?
999 Letsbe Avenue.

'I can't see anything wrong with you. It must be the drink.'
'Very well, doctor. I'll come back when you're sober.'

Hear about the posh new pub in Mayfair that sold Drambuie on draught?

'Have you tried our sausages, madam?'
'Yes – and found them guilty!'

'Could you see me across the road, constable?'
'Dunno, madam. I'll just hop over and look.'

'What are you going to be when you grow up and can only count to 10?'
'A boxing referee, miss.'

'Are you married, Charlie?'
'No, I've always been round-shouldered.'

Which monster has no luck?
The Luck Less Monster.

Hear about the farmer who called his pig Ink?
It kept running out of the pen.

'If you want work, I hear farmer McGregor is looking for a right-hand man.'
Tramp: 'Just my luck – I'm left-handed.'

'Willie's daughter married? Who's the lucky man?'
'Willie.'

'Did you want a plumber, lady?'
'Yes, I phoned you in January.'
'Wrong house, I'm afraid. The lady we're looking for phoned in November.'

Television will never take the place of newspapers. You can't swat flies with a TV set.

After an accident between a cement mixer and a prison van, police are looking for six hard men.

'Do any of your relatives come to see you in prison?'
'They don't have to – they're all here.'

'Are you sure this alarm clock is shock-proof? It's got to come face to face with the wife every morning.'

What swings about a sweet-shop yodelling?
Tarzipan.

Salesman: 'I've so much faith in this vacuum cleaner that if it doesn't pick up this handful of dirt, I'll eat it off the carpet myself.'
'Here's a spoon. We don't have any electricity.'

What's green, hairy and wears sunglasses?
A gooseberry on holiday.

Have you tried a French eggnog? Two egg yolks, two teaspoons of sugar and four jiggers of cognac in a tall, warm lass.

'A return ticket, please.'
'Where to, sir?'
'Back here, of course.'

'I don't want to go to school, mum. The teachers don't like me, and neither do the kids.'
'But you must go, son. After all, you're the headmaster.'

'And here,' said the guide, pointing to a brass plate on the deck, 'is where the gallant captain fell.'
'I'm not surprised – I nearly slipped on it myself.'

'Why have you stuck up your new wallpaper with tacks, Sandy?'
'You don't think I'm going to stay here all my life, do you?'

What's white and dashes through the desert with a bedpan?
Florence of Arabia.

'Do you have a village idiot?'
'No, we take it in turns.'

American tourist, lifting a melon: 'Is that the biggest apple you've got?'
Fruit seller: 'Don't finger the grapes, sir.'

Did you hear about the Irish maniokleptic? He walks backwards into shops and leaves things.

'This is an excellent clock. It'll go fifteen years without winding.'
'And how long will it go if I wind it?'

'Did you steal this carpet?'
'No, a lady gave it to me and told me to beat it.'

'Quick, doctor, I've been bitten by a snake. I've only a few seconds to live.'
'Right – I'll be with you in a minute.'

Did you hear about the mother python worried about her daughter? She was eighteen and never had a crush on anyone.

'Is that new scarecrow any good?'
'I'll say! It's given the crows such a scare they've brought back the seed they stole last week!'

Wife: 'Did you know most accidents happen in the kitchen?'
Husband: 'I know – I have to eat them.'

What's pink, lives at the bottom of the sea, and sings 'Give Me the Moonlight'?
Frankie Prawn.

My wife's so ugly that Peeping Toms knock on our door and ask us to close the curtains.

Hear about the chap who fell and trapped his nose in the tram-lines? They had to push him back to the depot to release him.

What did the cannibal have for lunch?
Baked beings on toast.

Definition of a true Scot: Someone who opens a bottle of whisky and throws the cork in the fire.

Our boarding-house was only a stone's throw from the beach. It was easy to find – all the windows were broken.

'Why did you take the whole day off yesterday, when I gave you only a half-day?'
'Well, sir, you always say never do things by halves.'

'Mum says could you lend us two slices of bread – and cut them with a jammy knife?'

What's green, leafy, and travels at 150mph?
A Lettuce Elan.

'I don't know whether to be a painter or a poet.'
'I suggest a painter.'
'You've seen one of my pictures?'
'No, I've read one of your poems.'

What did they call the baby bear that was born
bald?
Fredbear.

'How long has your mother-in-law been in hospital?'
'In three weeks' time, it will be a month.'

'That parrot you sold me won't say a word. You
promised it would repeat everything it heard.'
'So it would, sir, only it's stone deaf.'

'Please, sir, can you get punished for something
you haven't done?'
'Of course not.'
'Good – I haven't done my homework.'

'I've better news from school, Dad.'
'Did you pass your exam at last?'
'No, but I was top of those who failed.'

'What's your name?'
'Charles, madam.'
'I always address my chauffeurs by their surname.
What is it?'
'Darling, madam.'
'Drive on, Charles.'

'Waiter, there's a twig in my soup.'
'Hold on, sir, I'll call the branch manager.'

O'Reilly was killed in an accident, and Gogarty was appointed to break the news to his wife as tactfully as possible. She answered his knock on the door.
'Pardon me, are you the widow O'Reilly?'
'Certainly not.'
'Want ta' bet?'

Two boys in Hollywood were exchanging taunts.
'I bet my Dad can beat your Dad.'
'Yeah? My Dad *is* your Dad!'

Attendant in chamber of horrors: 'Kindly keep your wife moving, sir. We're stock-taking.'

'Do you call this a straight line?' yelled the Irish drill sergeant to the new recruits. 'Fall out and take a look at it!'

'Do you wish your office furnishings insured against theft?'
'Yes, all except the clock – everyone keeps an eye on that.'

'I've borrowed my neighbour's bagpipes.'
'But you can't play the bagpipes.'
'Neither can he while I've got them.'

What's black, dangerous and hides in trees?
A crow with a sub-machine gun.

'My husband seems a lot brighter today, nurse. He says he can't wait to get home to my cooking.'
'Yes, I'm afraid the anaesthetic hasn't worn off yet.'

How do you make a Peach Cordial?
Give her a mink coat.

'I'm sorry, madam, you can't bring that dog with you on this plane.'
'Why not? He's a Skye terrier.'

Did you hear about the man who spent his time kicking sand in men's faces on the beach? He sold chest expanders.

Hitch-hiker to car driver: 'Have you room for the five of us . . . or would you rather walk?'

Then there were the couple in the iron and steel business. She irons and he steals.

'Don't come down the ladder – I've taken it away.'
'Too late – I'm halfway down!'

'I said draw a man and a tent. Where's the man?'
'In the tent, miss.'

Judge: 'Have you a solicitor?'
Defendant: 'No, your honour, I've decided to tell the truth.'

If a man owned all the cows in Arabia, would he be a milk sheikh?

Paddy sat down in a restaurant on a Friday and asked the waiter: 'Have you any whale?'
'No, sir.'
'Shark, then?'
'Sorry.'
'Then bring me steak and chips. God knows I asked for fish.'

What perks do policemen get?
Truncheon vouchers.

'Give me a sentence with the word "judicious" in it.'
'Please, miss – hands that judicious can be soft as your face.'

'I've some good news for you, Mrs Brown.'
'I'm not married, doctor.'
'Then I've some bad news for you, Miss Brown.'

Tramp: 'I've asked for money, begged for money and cried for money.'
'Have you ever worked for it?'
'No, I'm going through the alphabet, and haven't reached "W" yet.'

An Irishman walked down the road punching women, kicking dogs and cursing children. He was going to confession, and didn't have enough material.

'My wife drives me to drink.'
'You're lucky – I have to walk.'

The greyhound had been a disaster at the track, and one owner suggested they throw him in the canal.
'Don't waste time,' said the other. 'Let's just run away from him.'

M.D.
LORNE

'I'd like to see some wedding rings.'
'Certainly, sir – eighteen carat?'
'No, I'm chewing a toffee, actually.'

What's fast, bald and takes pictures?
A Kojak Instamatic.

In the museum visitors' book, under the heading
'Reason for visit', someone wrote: 'Heavy shower'.

'Is this the first time you've been up before me?'
'Dunno, your honour – what time do you nor-
mally get up?'

'Waiter, have you frogs' legs?'
'No, sir, I always walk this way.'

'I thought you were supposed to come yesterday
to repair the doorbell?'
'I did, madam – I rang twice and got no answer.'

Note to tax man: 'Please accept enclosed £100, as my conscience keeps me awake at night. P.S. If I still can't sleep, I'll send the other £100.'

Then there was the Irishman who bought a TV dinner and listened to the radio.

And the Chinese reporter who burst into the office yelling: 'Hold the back page!'

And the butler who wrote a mystery story: the master did it.

'Steward – about that washing machine in my cabin. Every time I put clothes in, they disappear.'

'Knock-knock.'
'Who's there?'
'Ivor.'
'Ivor who?'
'Ivor you let me in the door, or I'll climb through the window.'

At last Charlie believes in superstition. He got lucky with Heather the other night.

What do you get if you cross a rabbit and an architect?
A burrow surveyor.

Incidentally, it's true carrots improve your sight. Well, you never see a rabbit with glasses.

Physiotherapist: 'It's going to rain today – I can feel it in your joints.'

I wouldn't say my husband was fat, but every time he gets measured for a suit, the tailor puts in for a travel allowance.

My wife's so ugly that she has to buy two tickets when she goes to the zoo – one to get in and one to get out.

One way to cut down on your drinking is to start using bigger ice cubes.

'What does "not transferable" mean on this ticket, Mick?'
'It means you won't be admitted if you don't go yourself.'

Hear about McTavish winning a holiday for two in Majorca? He went by himself twice.

Psychiatrist to patient: 'You're late – I was about to start without you!'

Sign in an Aberdeen hotel: 'Overcoats checked free during June, July and August.'

Young priest: 'He's confessed to stealing a crate of whisky. What'll I tell him?'
Old priest: 'We don't pay more than £1 a bottle.'

Barber: 'Your hair's getting grey, sir.'
'No wonder – hurry up!'

My wife has sinus trouble. She keeps saying 'Sinus a cheque.'

Then there was the Scot whose wife wanted something with diamonds in it for Christmas. So he bought her a pack of playing cards.

Officer (pointing to cigarette end on the parade ground): 'Is that yours, soldier?'
Private: 'That's all right, sir – you saw it first.'

What do you get when you cross a budgie with a lawn-mower?
Shredded tweat.

Psychiatrist **to** secretary: 'Just say we're terribly busy – not "It's a madhouse here!" '

Definition of an optimist: someone who goes into a restaurant and orders oysters, hoping he can pay for them with a pearl.

'Does this train stop at Dundalk?'
'That it does – get off three stations before I do and you'll be there.'

Cohen won £500,000 on the pools, but they didn't know how to tell him, as his heart was weak. Levy agreed to break the news to him gently, which he did with great tact.
'That's great news,' said Cohen. 'Tell me – why did you beat about the bush for so long?'
'We were afraid the shock might have been too much for you.'
'That was very kind of you, Levy, and let me tell you – I'm giving you half the money.'
And Levy dropped dead.

What do you call a snake with a bowler hat and umbrella?
A civil serpent.

What's soft, wet and sings 'When I'm Cleaning Windows'?
Chamois Davis Jr.

'What's your son going to be when he passes all his exams?'
'A pensioner.'

'Have you seen Sir John Gielgud as Titus Andronicus?'
'Dunno – how tight does Andronicus get?'

A priest stood next to a rabbi by the buffet at a fête. Selecting some of the cold meats, the priest joked, 'I wonder if I'll ever see you helping yourself to a plate of cold ham.'
'I probably will – at your wedding,' replied the rabbi.

Fat? When he gets his photo taken, they charge him at a group rate.

Then there was the Egyptian snake dancer who couldn't tell her asp from her elbow.

Elephant: 'Why are you so weak and tiny?'
Mouse: 'Well, I haven't been very well.'

One thing about McPherson – he always sticks up for his boss. He's a bill-poster.

'You've been watching me fishing for three hours. Why don't you take it up yourself?'
'I haven't the patience.'

'Your brother keeps borrowing from me and never pays it back.'
'Well, you see, he's saving up.'

'Lovely weather we're having,' said one fortune-teller to the other.
'Yes, reminds me of the summer of 1994.'

What do you get when you pour boiling water down a rabbit hole?
Hot cross bunnies.

M.D.
LORNE

A fellow walking down the street found a wage
packet. As he pocketed the money, his mate said,
'You're dead lucky, you are.'
'Lucky?' said the fellow. 'Just look at the tax I've
paid!'

Hear about the man who went to the money-
lender and asked for a loan? The clerk said, 'I'm
sorry, but the Loan Arranger isn't in.'
'Who do I see then?' asked the man.
And the clerk replied, 'Tonto.'

Then there was the Mafia football manager who
made an Irish player an offer he couldn't understand.

'You need glasses.'
'How do you know, doctor?'
'I could tell the moment you walked through the
door.'

And how about the East German pole-vaulting
champion who became the West German pole-
vaulting champion?

Two men were eating sandwiches in the factory.
One of them was jumping up and down.
Asked the foreman, 'What's wrong with him?'
His mate replied, 'He wants to go to the toilet.'
Foreman: 'Well, why doesn't he go?'
Mate: 'What – in his dinner hour?'

Incidentally, there hasn't been a single case of Asian 'flu in Liverpool for three years. The dockers have refused to handle it.

'Is that Dublin double-two double-two?'
'No, this is Dublin 2222.'
'Oh, sorry to have bothered you.'
'That's all right – the phone was ringing anyway.'

A dustman knocked on the door of this house and a Pakistani opened it. 'What do you want?' he asked.
'I've come about the bin,' said the dustman.
'I'm very sorry,' said the Pakistani. 'I let it yesterday.'

A weedy little fellow walked into a pub and shouted angrily, 'Who the hell painted my car bright pink?'
And a great big chap of seven feet stood up and said, 'I did.'
'Oh, well,' replied the little bloke, 'I just thought I'd tell you – the first coat is dry.'

A docker was walking out of the gates at Liverpool with a big pumpkin under his arm.
A policeman stopped him and asked, 'Where do you think you're going with that?'
'Oh, hell,' replied the docker, 'is it twelve o'clock already?'

A man on holiday in the Holy Land visited the Sea of Galilee. He asked a local fisherman, 'Can you take me across?'
'Certainly, sir,' replied the fisherman. 'It's £20 a trip.'
'Twenty pounds? That's a bit steep.'
'Remember, our Lord walked across here.'
'At those prices, I'm not surprised.'

Woman, deaf in left ear, with hearing aid, would like to meet man, deaf in right ear, with hearing aid. Object: stereo.

An actor was offered £2,000 a week to work on a new film. 'That's good pay,' he said. 'What's it called?'

'*Treasure Island*,' replied the director. 'I want you to play Long John Silver. Be on the set first thing on Tuesday morning.'

'For that money,' said the actor, 'I don't mind starting on Monday.'

'Not Monday,' said the director. 'Monday you're having your leg off.'

A Scot took his family into a restaurant in London, and they all ordered sausage, egg and chips. After the meal, there were two sausages on the plate.

The Scot told the waitress, 'I'll take them home for the dog.'

And one of the kids shouted, 'Whoopee – we're going to get a dog!'

'Mum, how do buffaloes make love?'

'I don't know, son – your Dad's a Mason.'

Two drunks were staggering home one night. One looked up and said, 'Is that the sun or the moon up there?'
And the other replied, 'I couldn't tell you . . . I don't live around here.'

A gorilla went into a pub, put £1 on the counter and asked for a pint of beer. The barman gave him a pint, 50p change and remarked, 'I hope you don't mind me staring at you, but we don't get many gorillas in here.'
'I'm not surprised,' said the gorilla, 'at 50p for a pint of bitter!'

Three men in a maternity hospital, waiting for news. The nurse comes in with a coloured baby and asks the first man, 'Is this yours?'
'No,' comes the reply.
She asks the second man, 'Is this yours?'
'No.'
Then the third man speaks up, 'It must be mine. That wife of mine burns everything!'

'Now, miss, what gear were you in at the time of the accident?'
'Let me see, officer – blue skirt, white jumper and tan boots.'

An Englishman, an Irishman and a Scotsman went on a cruise. Suddenly the liner struck a reef and started to sink.
'We'd better do something religious,' said the Englishman, and started to sing hymns. The Irishman led the prayers; and the Scotsman took a collection.

'Do you have any physical disabilities?' asked the army medical officer.
'Yes, I have – one leg is shorter than the other.'
'Don't worry about that. We'll post you to hill country.'

Did you hear about the vegetarian cannibal who would only eat Swedes?

If pop music went metric, would Mick Jagger sing with the Rolling Kilos?

Woman at Picasso exhibition: 'Attendant, can I have a word in your eye?'

Crossword fan: 'I've been trying to think of a word for two weeks.'
'How about "fortnight"?'

The phone rang in the maternity ward and an excited voice said, 'I'm bringing my wife – she's going to have a baby.'
'Is this her first baby?' asked the nurse.
'No,' came the reply, 'this is her husband.'

Optician: 'Can you read the bottom line of that chart?'
Pole: 'Read it? He's a friend of mine!'

Sign in Israeli barracks: 'Will privates kindly refrain from giving advice to officers.'

Then there was the Jewish kamikaze pilot who crashed on his brother-in-law's scrap yard.

Hear about the executive who advertised for a Girl Friday and was in Brighton with her by Sunday?

you get when you cross an elephant with
?
eat holes in the skirting board.

'My wife has this complex, doctor, about somebody stealing her clothes.'
'What makes you think that?'
'Well, she's even hired a chap to guard them. I
found him in the wardrobe last night.'

Hear about the two rabbits who got married and
went on a bunnymoon?

'Dear Mum, I was going to send you a couple of
quid for your birthday, but have already sealed
the envelope.'

'Your writing is terrible. What do you want to be
when you grow up?'
'A doctor, miss.'

Crowded? There were so many tourists they were
getting in each other's snapshots.

What sign does an Irish window cleaner put at the top of his ladder?
'*Stop!*'

'Why is this level-crossing gate half open?'
'Well, it's like this – we're half expecting a train.'

'As a top football player,' said the interviewer, 'you earn more money than the Prime Minister.'
'I should think so – I play a damn sight better than he does.'

Hear about the bank robber who decided to put the money back? He was generous to a vault.

Sign in restaurant: 'Forks and spoons aren't like medicine – to be taken after meals.'

Woman: 'If I give you a piece of pudding, will you promise not to come back?'
Tramp: 'You know your pudding better than I do, lady!'

'Do you have many lines in the play you're in?'
'No – I take the part of the husband.'

Who led 100,000 pigs up a hill and then back down again?
The Grand Old Duke of Pork.

What do you call a nun with a wooden leg?
Hopalong Chastity.

'Your suit will be ready in three months, sir.'
'Three months? Why, it took only six days to make the whole world.'
'Yes – and have you noticed the state it's in?'

Then there was the Irishman who refused to buy a pocket calculator. He already knew how many pockets he had.

Goldberg and Finkelstein were partners. While they were lunching, Goldberg shouted, 'My God, I left the safe open!'
'Don't worry,' said Finkelstein, 'we're both here.'

'I hope as a typist you understand the importance of punctuation.'
'Don't worry, sir – I always get to work on time.'

Constable: 'Your rear light's not working.'
Motorist: 'I'll give it a kick – there!'
Constable: 'Now kick your windscreen – your road tax is out of date.'

'I'm very sorry, lady, but I've just run over your cat. I'd like to replace it.'
'How are you at catching mice?'

When Charlie sent his photograph to a Lonely Hearts club, back came the reply, 'We're not that lonely.'

Did you hear about the man who took up lion-taming for a living? He used to be a teacher, but he lost his nerve.

'Did you enjoy your first day at school?'
'Yes, but I've to go back tomorrow.'

'How do you mean – your school is well thought of by everyone?'
'Well, it's approved.'

'This banana diet is having an odd effect on me, doctor.'
'For the last time, will you stop scratching and come down from those curtains!'

The village idiot sat dangling a fishing line down a manhole. The new parson gave him 50p and asked kindly, 'How many have you caught today?'
'You be the tenth,' replied the yokel.

Pools winner: 'Dine with the captain? I spend all this money on a luxury cruise and they expect me to eat with the crew!'

'Waiter, can I have some undercooked chips, cold beans and a fried egg coated in grease?'
'I'm sorry, sir, but we couldn't possibly give you anything like that.'
'Why not? That's what you served up yesterday.'

Inscription on the tombstone of a hypochondriac: 'See – I *told* you I was ill.'

'But, Angus, that isn't our baby.'
'Shut up, woman – it's a better pram.'

'Remember, politeness costs nothing.'
'Doesn't it? Try putting "I remain your obedient servant" at the end of a telegram.'

'I've come to collect the reward for returning your budgie.'
'But that's not a budgie – it's a cat.'
'I know, but the budgie's inside it.'

Woman, trying on mink coat: 'If my husband doesn't like it, will you refuse to take it back?'

Two Irishmen, breaking out of jail, noticed a spotlight. 'Let's turn it on,' said one, 'then we can point it outwards and slide down the beam.' 'Not likely,' said the other. 'We might get halfway down and somebody switches it off.'

Politician: 'I was born an Englishman and I'll die an Englishman.'
Scot in audience: 'Ach, have ye nae ambition?'

Definition of a bigamist: a man who makes the same mistake twice.

Then there was the Irishman who went bankrupt selling lucky charms.

'Madam, your dog's been chasing a man on a bicycle.'
'Nonsense, officer, my dog can't ride a bicycle.'

Hear about the woman who got rid of fifteen stone of ugly, excess fat? She divorced him.

What did the coke sing to the coal?
What kind of fuel am I?

My mother-in-law ugly? When a tear rolled down her cheek, it took one look at her face and rolled straight back up again.

Hear about the cannibals converted to Christianity by a Catholic missionary? Now they only eat fishermen on Fridays.

'Have you any dogs going cheap?'
'Sorry, sir, all our dogs go woof.'

'To which family does the whale belong?'
'Don't know, sir. No family near us has one.'

Museum curator: 'That's a 5,000-year-old gold vase you've just smashed.'
'Thank heaven – I thought it was a new one!'

What's chocolate outside, peanut inside and sings hymns?
A Sunday School Treet.

'What would you like for your birthday?' asked Hymie.
'Well,' said his wife, 'I've got a mink coat, a car and plenty of diamonds. I'd like £1,000.'
'And where do you think I'll get £1,000 wholesale?'

Poor? We were so poor, one of my brothers was made in Hong Kong.

Then there was the man who kept a portrait of his mother-in-law above the fireplace. It kept the children away from the fire.

'Doctor, doctor, my hand won't stop shaking.'
'Do you drink a lot?'
'No – I spill most of it.'

What happens to ducks who fly upside down?
They quack up.

'How did you get those scars on the top of your nose?'
'From glasses.'
'Why don't you try contact lenses?'
'They don't hold enough beer.'

Gypsy: 'Buy a lucky charm, lady? Take away the curse I just put on your house.'

A football fan phoned Albion Rovers ground to ask what time the match started that day.
'What time can you get here?' came the reply.

'Nurse, what would it take to make you give me a kiss?'
'Chloroform.'

One waitress to another: 'I always start the day with a smile – and get it over with.'

'You're dancing with me tonight, and I suppose tomorrow you'll make a date with some other man.'
'Yes – my chiropodist.'

A wise husband buys his wife such fine china that she won't trust him to wash up the dishes.

'The specialist promised to put me on my feet in six weeks – and he did. I had to sell my car to pay his bill.'

My wife is so houseproud she even puts newspaper under the cuckoo clock.

Isaac was dying, and the family gathered round his bedside. 'Mama,' he whispered.
'I'm here, Isaac.'
'Miriam,' he sighed.
'I'm here, Papa.'
'Solly!'
'Here, Papa.'
'Jacob?'
'I'm here, too, Papa.'
'Then who the hell is minding the shop?'

'Doctor, my wife complains I'm eating like a horse.'
'Would you mind removing that nosebag? I can't hear a word you're saying.'

'Did you get through the French customs all right?'
'Not all of them – I was only in Paris two days.'

Two escaped lions walked along the seafront at Blackpool. Said one: 'Not much of a crowd for a Bank Holiday.'

Sign on a church notice board: 'Gossip runs down more people than cars.'

Coalman to housewife: 'Your parrot's a good talker.'
Parrot: 'I can count, too – put another bag in.'

Who are the biggest ice-cream makers in Israel?
Walls of Jericho.

This next turn, ladies and gentlemen, has been thrown off more stages than John Wayne.

On his first lesson a golfer hit the ball off the course. It landed on the main road and hit a bus driver, causing a pile-up which injured twenty-seven people.
'What shall I do?' asked the golfer.
'Don't panic,' replied the instructor. 'Try holding your thumb a bit lower down . . .'

'How did you find your steak, sir?'
'Easy – I'm a detective.'

Then there was the Irish housewife who was going to make rhubarb tart, but couldn't find a dish long enough.

Overheard in pub: 'I'm the boss in my house, all right – nobody tells *me* how to wash the dishes!'

'I always tell my Mum any bad news when "Crossroads" is on. Then all she says is "Shhhh"!'

'Waiter, how come you bring me a lobster with only one claw?'
'I'm sorry, sir, but it was in a fight.'
'Well, take it away and bring me the winner.'

Attendant at boating lake: 'Come in, number 91. Come in, number 91. Are you in trouble, number 16?'

'Tell me – do you have trouble making up your mind?'
'Well, yes and no, doctor.'

Who invented the fireplace?
Alfred the Grate.

Hear about the dentist who married a manicurist? They've been fighting tooth and nail ever since.

We regret the butcher accidentally backed into the bacon slicer. As a result, we've got a little behind with your orders.

El Al pilot: 'We are now flying at 50,000 feet . . .
but, to you, 45,000.'

British Airways pilot: 'We are now about to land
at Belfast airport. Watches should be put back
three hundred years.'

Shady? He's the only man I know whose luncheon
vouchers bounce.

'Why do you say George is a born executive?'
'His father owns the business.'

If a fool and his money are soon parted, how does
a fool and his money get together in the first
place?

'I'm thinking of buying a Rolls-Royce. Can you
tell me the annual cost of running one?'
'Anyone who needs to ask a question like that,
sir, can't afford one.'

LORNE

'Excuse me, I'm a stranger here. Where's the nearest boozer?'
'You're looking at him.'

Hear about the illegitimate Rice Krispie?
Snap, crackle, no pop.

'Don't you find a baby brightens up the house wonderfully?'
'Quite true – we have the light on most of the night.'

'Talk about a heatwave. I saw a greyhound chasing a hare and they were both walking.'

'These mothballs you sold me are no good.'
'Why not?'
'I haven't hit a single moth with them.'

Then there was the farmer who went over his spud field with a heavy roller. He was raising mashed potatoes.

An Irishman went to buy a collar for his dog, but
wasn't too sure of the size.
'Bring him in and we'll fit him,' said the assistant.
'Oh, I couldn't do that – it's for his birthday and
I want it to be a surprise.'

A man went into a barber's and asked for a Tom
Jones haircut. The barber gave him a short back
and sides.
'Tom Jones doesn't have his hair cut like that,'
protested the man.
'He does if he comes in here,' replied the barber.

'Doctor, my wife's dislocated her jaw. If you're
passing in the next month or two, would you
mind looking in?'

The secret of gardening success? Trowel and
error.

'A pair of kippers, please.'
'Sorry, haven't a pair left.'
'Don't worry. Give me two odd ones – the wife'll
never know the difference.'

Hear about the man who crossed a carrier pigeon with a parrot so it could deliver messages verbally?

The first time he tried it out, the bird turned up two hours late. 'What kept you?' asked the man. 'It was such a lovely day,' replied the bird, 'I decided to walk.'

'Doctor, I feel aches and pains all over.'
'You're just a little stiff.'

'I dreamt last night I was talking to the wisest man in the world.'
'Really? What did I say?'

Murphy held up a ship launching for three days. He wouldn't let go of the bottle.

'Doctor, I keep thinking there are two of me.'
'Don't both speak at once.'

'There goes eight bells, madam,' said the ship's officer. 'It's my watch below.'
'Fancy a watch striking as loudly as that!'

'Do you enjoy Kipling?'
'Don't know – I've never kippled.'

Sultan in harem: 'Your eyes are like stars that shine in the night, your lips taste like wine. Pass it on.'

Expectant father: 'If it's a boy, let's call him John. If it's a girl, let's call her Jane. And if it's twins, let's call it a day.'

What do you call a neurotic octopus?
A crazy, mixed-up squid.

Old lady to pilot: 'You *will* bring me down safely, won't you?'
'Don't worry, lady, I've never left anybody up there yet.'

'When ye get tae the door on New Year's Eve, kick twice and I'll know who it is.'
'Haven't you a doorbell or knocker?'
'Aye, but ye'll no' be coming empty-handed, will ye?'

'My dear, this sale coat was a real bargain. I got it for a ridiculous figure.'
'So I see.'

Notice in an Edinburgh travel agent: 'Please do us a favour and go away.'

For sale: unused chest expander. Cannot get lid off box.

One gardener to another: 'You should get my missus to talk to that bush . . . she'd drive anything up the wall.'

For years we couldn't afford a sledge in winter. We used to slide down hills on my sister.

High Court judge: 'Time and again, I hear of young men and women devoted to drinking, dancing and even gambling . . . time that would be much better spent in bed.'

'If you don't get through any more work next week, I'll have to hire another boy.'
'Thank you very much, sir – I could do with some help.'

The Animals were beating the Insects 20–0 at football, until the centipede came on half an hour from time and helped the Insects to a 75–20 win. It would have come on sooner, but it was lacing up its boots.

Big? When she hung her knickers on the line we lost an hour's daylight.

'Do you believe in striking children?'
'Only in self-defence.'

What did the Irishman say when he saw ballerinas on their toes for the first time?
They'd be better just getting taller girls.

Heavy traffic? One woman had to abandon her car and continue her driving test on foot.

'I think I've broken my leg, sarge.'
'Well, don't waste time down there – do some press-ups!'

What do you get when you cross a cocoa bean with an elk?
A chocolate moose.

Wife, with camera, to hubby: 'Well, don't just stand there – get into focus!'

A drunken sailor was asked why he was walking with one foot on the pavement and the other in the gutter.
'Is that what I'm doing?' he replied. 'Thank heaven – I thought I was a cripple.'

'Now, Tommy, tell me where you buried Dad in
the sand – he's got the train tickets.'

Young Paddy persuaded his Dad to buy him a
drum. He promised to play it only when he was
asleep.

Honest? McTavish worked for two years at the
public baths and never once took a bath.

Barber: 'Have you been here before?'
'Yes, once.'
'Funny – I don't remember your face.'
'No, it's healed up since then.'

'I'm going to the doctor – I don't like the look of
my wife.'
'I'll come with you – I hate the sight of mine.'

'I hear she had her husband cremated.'
'Isn't that typical? Some of us can't get a husband
for love nor money – others have husbands to
burn.'

What did the sparrow say to the starling?
I've just made a deposit on a new Ford.

A man, released from jail after twenty years, found a receipt for a pair of shoes he had taken to be repaired the day he went away. So on the off-chance, he went in to the old cobbler, explained about the ticket and asked if he still had the shoes.
The cobbler looked at the ticket. 'Were they brown with a bit of stitching on the toecaps?'
'That's right.'
'You wanted them soled and heeled?'
'Yes, I did.'
'Be ready Wednesday.'

'Give it to me straight, doctor, how long have I got?'
'It's difficult to say, but I wouldn't buy any long-players.'

'Were you pleased with the woolly vest I sent you for Christmas?'
'Tickled pink, auntie.'

Notice in a Glasgow store: 'Ears pierced while you wait.'

New Year is a time for making resolutions. Last year, I resolved to give up drink, gambling and women. It was the most miserable forenoon I've ever spent. 

Then there was the bride who spent the first night of her honeymoon looking out of the window. Her mother had told her it would be the most wonderful night of her life, and she didn't want to miss a minute of it.

'Doctor, I'm at my wit's end.'
'Well, you haven't had to travel far.'

Dumb? When she saw me off at the station, she put on a pair of platform shoes.

Fortune teller: 'I see you as a leader of a vast number of men.'
Referee: 'Have I a good start?'

CORNE

'Mum, I don't like cheese with holes in it.'
'Stop being fussy. Eat the cheese and leave the holes at the side of your plate.'

Psychiatrist: 'You're suffering from loss of memory. My fee is 50 guineas – in advance.'

Why do polar bears have fur coats?
They'd look funny in tweed ones.

Where do parrots with three A-levels go?
A polly technic.

Murphy was so delighted to win a first-ever cup winners' gold medal that he had it silver-plated.

'Money doesn't buy happiness.'
'No, but it lets you be miserable in comfort.'

'Do you think it would be wrong of me to play golf on the Sabbath, vicar?'
'The way you play it's a sin any day of the week.'

Trainer: 'Couldn't you have gone any faster?'
Jockey: 'Yes, but the rules say I must stay with the horse.'

If opportunity knocked, my husband would complain about the noise.

'What would you do if you were in my shoes?'
'Clean them!'

For sale: twin beds, one hardly used.

Unlucky? He bought a suit with two pairs of trousers and burnt a hole in the jacket.

'This beer's terrible – I'll be glad when I've had enough!'

All my wife wants for her birthday are a few
cards. An American Express card, a Barclay-
card . . .

A man was walking round a building site, when
he saw three labourers holding hands and dancing
round a hole in the ground.
'What's up?' he asked the foreman. 'Is it somebody's birthday?'
'No,' replied the foreman. 'It's the third anniver-
sary of the hole.'

'He must have been a very keen golfer,' said the
vicar at the cemetery. 'Look at the golf clubs and
golf shoes on the coffin.'
'Oh, no,' said a mourner. 'Those belong to one of
the bearers.'

'What did your husband say when you smashed
the new car?'
'Shall I leave out the swear words?'
'Of course.'
'He didn't say a word.'

'Waiter, do I have to sit here until I starve?'
'Oh, no, sir – we close at six.'

Bridget was appalled when the doctor told her she was expecting twins.
'Now, let me see,' she mused. 'When did I go on a double date?'

Cohen walked into a delicatessen, bought some tomatoes and asked carelessly: 'By the way, how much is that bacon?'
Just then, there was a terrific flash of lightning and a clap of thunder. 'Look,' said Cohen, peering up to the heavens in protest, 'I was only *asking*!'

'Waiter, a mutton chop and chips, please. And make the chop lean.'
'Certainly, sir – which way?'

'Is your watchdog any good, Paddy?'
'Oh, yes! If you hear a suspicious noise at night, you've only to wake him and he barks!'

'What do you think of marriage as an institution?'
'Great – for people who like living in institutions.'

'Can you guarantee, doctor, that if I give up drinking, smoking and sex, I will live longer?'
'No, but it will seem longer.'

'Could I speak to the landlord, please?'
'Speaking.'
'It's about the roof.'
'Yes?'
'We'd like one.'

A young couple went to the building society. 'I earn £30 a week,' said the husband. 'How do we stand for a mortgage?'
'You don't,' came the reply, 'you grovel.'

A man was walking along a dimly lit street, when he was stopped by a stranger.
'What do you want?' asked the man nervously.
'Would you be so kind,' said the stranger, 'as to help a poor, unfortunate fellow who's hungry and out of work? All I have in the world is this gun.'

An Irish decorator was painting a house like mad.
'Why all the rush?' asked the owner.
'Well, you see, the paint's running low, and I want to finish the job before it's all done.'

The husband came home from work the first day after the honeymoon, and found his wife crying her eyes out in front of the new washing-machine.
'Why, darling, whatever's the matter?' he asked.
'I've tried everything,' she sobbed, 'and I still can't get a picture on this television.'

'How say you? Are you guilty or not guilty?'
'I can't answer till I've heard the evidence.'

News flash: the Post Office has just bought a fleet of detector vans with big bones on the roof to catch up on people who haven't got dog licences.

'I don't understand why they've put statues on that building.'
'They're not statues – they're bricklayers.'

'Waiter, there's a dead fly in my soup.'
'Not so loud, sir, or they'll all want one.'

'I can't possibly play the three parts you've given me in this play.'
'Why not?'
'Well, in the last act, I've to fight with myself and then rush in and separate the two of us!'

'Doctor, I keep talking to myself.'
'I wondered why you were looking so bored!'

'Mummy, do you and Daddy have sexual relations?'
'Yes, dear, why do you ask?'
'Well, why haven't I met any of them?'

Then there was the old maid who went for a tramp in the woods. He got away.

I wouldn't say my wife was a bad cook, but our dustbin has ulcers.

A newcomer at the Pearly Gates knocked for admission.
'Who's there?' asked St Peter.
'It is I,' came the reply.
'Go to hell – we've too many English professors here already!'

I gave my mother-in-law a waterproof, shock-proof, anti-magnetic, unbreakable watch. She went and lost it.

A man asked a labourer how much he got for banging his hammer down.
'Nothing, sir,' he answered. 'It goes down itself. I get paid for lifting it up.'

'Waiter, there's a fly in my soup.'
'No, sir, that's the chef . . . the last customer was a witch doctor.'

'I've just lost my dog.'
'Why don't you put an advert in the paper?'
'Don't be silly, it can't read.'

LORNE

'Is your ice-cream pure?'
'As pure as the girl of your dreams.'
'Give me some popcorn.'

Mrs Cohen: 'Don't tell a soul, but I'm having an affair.'
Mrs Levy: 'Really? Who's doing the catering?'

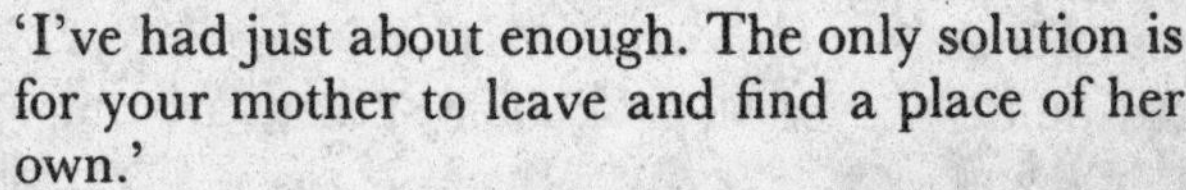

'I've had just about enough. The only solution is for your mother to leave and find a place of her own.'
'My mother? I thought she was *your* mother!'

'This new hearing aid is so small that nobody notices it.'
'That's great. How much did it cost?'
'Half-past four.'

'How are you and your new wife getting on?'
'Not too good, vicar. I'm afraid we've separated.'
'But you took her for better or worse.'
'Yes, but she was worse than I took her for.'

Two Irishmen hired a boat, went fishing, and caught lots of fish. 'This is a good place,' said one. 'It'd be good to have another go tomorrow, but we'll never find it again.'
'Don't worry,' said the other, 'I've marked the side of the boat with a cross.'
'That's no good. We may not get the same boat tomorrow.'

'I say, waiter, the flies are very thick around here.'
'I wouldn't say that, sir – some of them are quite intelligent.'

Sign in an undertaker's: 'Join our Christmas Club'.

A man lost his ear and asked a friend to help him look for it. After searching for a while, the friend found an ear and told his friend.
'That's not my ear,' said the man. 'Mine had a pencil behind it.'

Then there was the Irishman who broke into a depot to pinch a bus to get home. He was out of luck – there wasn't a No. 15 there.

Alsatian: 'This snow freezes my paws.'
Dachshund: 'I should be so lucky.'

'Doctor, I keep thinking I'm a bottle of gin.'
'What you need is a little tonic.'

I wouldn't say she was big, but she used to kick-start jumbo jets.

'There's a postman at the door with a parcel marked COD.'
'Tell him to take it back – I ordered haddock.'

Irish knock-knock.
'Who's there?'
'O'Mally.'
'O'Mally who?'
'Charlie's Angels.'

When fire broke out in the Chelsea boardroom, a director shouted, 'Quick, save the cups!' And everyone ran to the canteen.

'There's a man outside to see you with a funny face.'
'Tell him I've got one.'

'Have you ever had this complaint before?'
'Yes, doctor, about two years ago.'
'Well . . . er . . . you've got it again.'

'This is your room,' said the landlady. 'Any complaints?'
'Well, the window's a bit small . . . wouldn't be much use in an emergency.'
'There won't be an emergency. My terms are cash in advance.'

'I had to change my seat five times at the cinema last night, Mary.'
'Why? Did some chap bother you?'
'Yes, eventually.'

A young woman went into a bank and asked to withdraw some money.

'Can you identify yourself?' asked the cashier.

The woman opened her handbag, looked in a mirror, and said, 'Yes, it's me all right.'

'Ah,' said the businessman, 'what a wonderful weekend we had in Brighton. Can you ever forget it?'

'What's it worth?' asked the secretary.

'Isn't £60 a bit much for a sweater?'

'Certainly not, sir. It's all wool, shorn from a unique breed of sheep, whose habitat is the most inaccessible region of the Himalayas. It's a truly beautiful yarn.'

'Yes – and you tell it well, too!'

Then there was the couple who decided to call their baby Bill, as he was due at the end of the month.

'Waiter, there's a dead fly in my wine.'

'Well, you did ask for something with a little body in it.'

'This parrot is very religious. If you pull his right leg, he says the Lord's Prayer, and if you pull his left leg, he recites the Twenty-third Psalm.'
'What happens if you pull both legs?'
'I fall flat on my back,' said the parrot.

Who didn't invent aeroplanes?
The Wrong Brothers.

'I've nothing for you today,' said the man to the beggar. 'Come back tomorrow.'
'Very well,' came the reply, 'but I've lost a lot of money giving credit that way.'

'Tell me, who's the oldest inhabitant in this village?'
'We 'aven't got one now, sir. He died three weeks ago.'

'Doctor, I'm suffering from insomnia.'
'Go home and sleep it off.'

'May I try on that check suit in the window?'
'Certainly, sir – but we do have a changing room.'

A man paid £500 for a talking dog. He took it
home to show his friend, who offered him 10–1 it
wouldn't say a word.
'Right,' said the owner and did everything in his
power to make the dog talk. Nothing.
His friend roared with laughter, pocketed his
winnings and left.
The owner turned on the dog. 'Why didn't you
say something, you stupid animal?'
'Not so much of the stupid,' replied the dog.
'Think of the odds you'll get next time.'

'Why is this station called Fish Hook?'
'It's at the end of the line.'

Definition of a bore: someone who, when you ask
him how he is, tells you.

'How often, pilot, do aircraft of this type crash?'
'Only once, madam.'

A flea spent the evening in a pub drinking Scotch. At closing time he hopped out into the street, leapt in the air and fell flat on his face. 'Damn,' he said, 'someone's moved my dog.'

'Do you know I fought more than an hour with that salmon you're eating?'
'Yes, why someone can't design an efficient tin-opener, I don't know.'

'My mother-in-law has disappeared.'
'Have you given her description to the police?'
'No – they'd never believe me.'

'Commissionaire – call me a taxi!'
'Certainly, sir. You're a taxi.'

'Doctor, I'm fed up being only three feet tall.'
'You'll just have to learn to be a little patient.'

For sale. Honeymoon cottage. Sleeps three.

Hear about the cannibal who got married and, at the reception, toasted his mother-in-law?

'When the barometer falls, what does that tell us?'
'The nail's come out of the wall, miss.'

If rabbits' feet are so lucky, how come so many rabbits keep losing them?

Then there was the man who gave up mending ladders in stockings. He couldn't stand tights.

'I haven't eaten for three days, lady.'
'My, I wish I had your will-power.'

'Waiter, do you have frogs' legs?'
'Yes, sir.'
'Well, hop over the counter and get me a sandwich.'

'What did you do on earth?' asked St Peter.
'I was a professional footballer.'
'Oh, and where are your boots?'
'I left them on earth.'
'Well, hurry back and get them – we're playing Hell tonight.'

A couple were watching the Open golf on television, when the wife went to turn the sound up. 'Sssh,' said the husband, 'not while he's putting.'

'Doctor, my shins are hacked to pieces.'
'So they are. What have you been playing – soccer or rugby?'
'Neither – bridge.'

'What can you see out of that window?' asked the optician.
'I can only see the sun.'
'Well, how far do you want to see?'

'How many new-laid eggs have we in stock, boy?'
'Oh, about enough to last us six weeks, sir.'

'Now, children, I hope you have a nice holiday
and come back to school with a little sense in
your heads.'
'Same to you, miss!'

'My wife said I was to ask for a rise, sir.'
'Right – I'll ask my wife if I can give you one.'

'Why didn't you shave this morning, Private
Jones?'
'Well, sarge, there were eight of us sharing the
same mirror this morning, and I must have
shaved the wrong face.'

Two flies were playing football in a saucer. Said
one: 'We'll have to do better than this – we're
playing in the cup next week.'

'This essay on "My Dog" is word for word the
same as your sister's.'
'I know, sir – it's the same dog.'

'I don't like that cold of yours.'
'I'm sorry, doctor, it's the best I've got.'

'Dad, is it true we're descended from monkeys?'
'Dunno, son. I never met any of your mother's relations.'

'You told me this dog was splendid for rats, but, in two weeks, it hasn't caught one.'
'Well, isn't that splendid for rats?'

'I tell you, Bessie, things aren't going well with the Goldbergs.'
'What makes you say that?'
'I saw both their daughters playing on the one piano!'

'Are those eggs fresh?'
'Feel the eggs, Charlie, and see if they're cool enough to sell yet.'

'Why are the curtains drawn, doctor?' asked the man after his operation. 'Is it night-time already?' 'No, there's a fire across the road, and I didn't want you to wake up and think the operation hadn't been successful.'

114

LORNE

'Foul,' said the referee, when the elephant stamped
on the mouse in a football match.
'Sorry, ref,' said the elephant. 'I only meant to
trip him.'

'Did the butcher have pigs' feet, Billy?'
'I couldn't see, Mum – he had his shoes on.'

'Waiter, this soup plate's still wet.'
'That, sir, is your soup.'

'Does your husband talk in his sleep?'
'No, it's so exasperating – he just grins.'

'Hello, Archie. Fishing?'
'Naw – drownin' worms.'

'You're OK. You'll live to be 70.'
'But I am 70, doctor.'
'There – what did I tell you?'

'I've two flowers in my garden. One is amnesia and I've forgotten the other.'

'Dad, when did Burns Night start?'
'The first dinner after I married your mother.'

'Do you think I should put more fire in my poetry?'
'No, I think you should put more of your poetry in the fire.'

'Are these seeds quick growing?'
'Yes, sir, after planting, I advise you to jump clear.'

Then there was the hedgehog that went steady with a scrubbing brush.

'I'd like some poison for mice, please.'
'Have you tried Boots, sir?'
'I want to poison them – not kick them to death.'

'Steward – I must complain. A sailor came into my cabin last night.'
'What do you expect for tourist class, madam – the captain?'

A man took a photograph of his son to the chemist. 'I'd like you to enlarge this for me,' he said, 'and would it be possible to remove his hat?'
'Certainly, sir, but tell me – which side does your son part his hair?'
'Oh, come now – you'll see that when you take his hat off.'

'Doctor, can you give me something to make me sweat?'
'Yes. Here's a signing-off note.'

'Who was that lady I saw you with last night?'
'That was no lady – that was my brother . . . he always dresses that way.'

'It appears you are not telling the truth, my man.'
'How do you mean, your honour?'
'You told us you had only one brother, whereas your sister says she has two.'

My mother-in-law makes her own yoghourt. She buys a bottle of milk and stares at it for a couple of minutes.

Brown lost two stone in a fortnight. 'How did you do it?' asked Smith.
'I went to Dr Jones and he gave me these amazing tablets. Every night I dream I'm on a desert island chasing hundreds of native girls. When I wake up, I've lost another couple of pounds.'
So Smith rushed off to Dr Jones, got the tablets and started taking them. Within a week he was back, thinner but disgruntled.
'What's the matter?' asked the doctor. 'You're losing weight, aren't you?'
'Yes,' replied Smith, 'but my friend has this wonderful dream about chasing native girls. I dream I'm on a desert island, but it's full of cannibals, who chase me all night.'
'It's quite simple,' explained Dr Jones. 'Your friend's a private patient – you're on the National Health.'

What's wrapped in greaseproof paper and hangs around French cathedrals?
The Lunchpack of Notre Dame.

Fat man: 'You look as though you've been through a famine.'
Thin man: 'You look as though you'd caused it.'

'What would you be charging,' asked Murphy, 'to put a death notice in your paper?'
'50p an inch.'
'Glory be – and me brother was six feet tall!'

Who wrote *Great Eggspectations*?
Charles Chickens.

Then there was the pop group that called themselves Instant Potato. They had a Smash hit.

'Our rates are £5 a night, bed and breakfast, or £4 if you make your own bed.'
'Very well, I'll make the bed.'
'Here's the saw and hammer – help yourself to some nails.'

Then there was the Aberdeen man who went to Torquay alone on his honeymoon. His wife had been there before.

'Waiter, this steak is so tough, I can't even cut it. Take it away and bring me another.'
'Sorry, sir, I can't do that. You've bent it.'

There's only one difference between McTavish and a coconut. You can get a drink out of a coconut.

He who laughs last is trying to think of a double meaning.

'Has your dog a pedigree?'
'Well, he has on his mother's side. And his father comes from a very good neighbourhood.'

'Waiter, do you ever have a clean tablecloth?'
'I couldn't say, sir – I've only been here a year.'

'How do you know when winter is approaching?'
'Please, sir, it begins to get late earlier.'

A Hollywood film star returned to Britain to make a film after an absence of ten years. She particularly asked that she be photographed by the same cameraman as before.

When she saw the rushes, she complained, 'These are not nearly as good as the ones you took of me last time.'

'I know,' replied the cameraman, 'but, remember, I'm ten years older.'

'What happens to a footballer if his eyesight fails, Dad?'

'He becomes a referee.'

'Why are you cleaning the inside of the windows, Bridget, but not the outside?'

'Well, ma'am, that way you can look out, but the folk outside can't look in.'

'Give me a sentence with the word "centimetre" in it.'

'Please, miss – my aunt was coming home from her holidays and I was centimetre.'

What's bright yellow and dangerous?
Shark-infested custard.

The priests were playing the rabbis at football, and the rabbis won 15–0. The priests got together and decided to have a return match. 'This time we'll sign up a new centre-forward . . . Father Cruyff,' they said.
So they did, and finished up losing 7–1. One of the priests rang the monastery to tell the bad news. 'You're joking,' said the priest in charge. 'Who scored for us?'
'Father Cruyff,' replied the priest.
'And who scored for them?'
'Rabbi Keegan and Rabbi Dalglish.'

'I'm writing my autobiography, to be published posthumously.'
'I can't wait to read it.'

A cannibal who owned a restaurant in the jungle put up the menu for the day:

Fried Scot –	50p
Fried Englishman –	50p
Fried Irishman –	50p
Fried hippy –	£1.95

Asked a customer: 'Why do you charge so much for the hippy?'
Replied the cannibal: 'Have you ever tried to clean one?'

'Have you anything to say before sentence is passed?'
'Yes, as God is my judge, I am innocent.'
'He isn't; I am; you aren't; six months.'

'May I take you home from the dance? I like to take experienced girls home.'
'But I'm not experienced.'
'You're not home yet!'

A commuter asked a ticket collector at Victoria Station when the next train was to Brighton.
'Six forty-five,' was the reply.
'Are you sure?'
'Well, if you doubt me, ask my mate over there.'
So the commuter approached the West Indian ticket collector and asked *him* the time of the next train to Brighton.
'Six forty-five, sir,' came the answer. 'Now you have it in black and white.'

A traveller passing through a small Irish town saw a funeral going down the main street. 'Who died?' he asked a passer-by.
'I can't say for sure,' came the reply, 'but I think it's the one in the hearse.'

A visitor to New Mexico was commenting on the lack of rain. 'Doesn't it *ever* rain here?' he asked a sun-browned native.

'Well,' came the reply. 'Do you remember the story of Noah and the Ark, and how it rained forty days and forty nights?'

'Yes, I do.'

'Well, we got half an inch that time.'

Then there was the cannibal who came home to find his wife chopping up snakes and a very small man.

'Oh, no,' he groaned, 'not snake and pygmy pie *again*!'

Loudspeaker announcement on a London to Glasgow train: 'Ladies and gentlemen, you are warned that lunch will be served shortly.'

'Did you hear about Murphy trying to drown himself in a vat of Guinness?'

'No – what happened?'

'Three men jumped in to save him, but he fought them off.'

'I came in answer to your advert for a handyman.'
'Good – go and help lay some bricks.'
'I'm sorry – I can't lay bricks.'
'Then mix some concrete for the path.'
'I can't mix concrete.'
'Well, saw some wood then.'
'I'm afraid I don't know how to saw.'
'Tell me – what's so handy about you?'
'I live just round the corner.'

Definition of an elephant: a mouse built according to Government specifications.

'Excuse me, sir, you don't seem to have any rear lights on your car.'
'Never mind the car, officer – where's my flipping caravan?'

'Who was that on the phone?' asked the wife.
'It was a wrong number, dear. Some chap looking for the Met Office . . . wanted to know if the coast was clear.'

What did they give the man who invented door knockers?
The No Bell Prize.

Hear about the businessman who marketed a new cure for headaches called Nothing? He claimed Nothing acts faster than Anadin.

'Did you know your wife fell out of the car four miles back?'
'Thank God for that, officer – I thought I'd gone deaf!'

'Knock-knock.'
'Who's there?'
'Mahatma.'
'Mahatma who?'
'Mahatma coat, please . . . that's the end of the book!'